Card Craft

Create your own greeting
cards with over 80 projects

Card Craft

Create your own greeting
cards with over 80 projects

Published in 2013
by Igloo Books Ltd
Cottage Farm
Sywell
NN6 0BJ
www.igloobooks.com

FIR003 0213
2 4 6 8 10 9 7 5 3 1
ISBN 978-1-78197-315-8

Printed and manufactured in China

Contents

Introduction

Cards are the perfect way to express a wide variety of sentiments. Happy Birthday, Congratulations, Get Well Soon, every occasion can be marked with a beautiful card. Cards made by hand add a deeper level of charm, taking the time to carefully construct something lovely and personal is appreciated by both the maker and the receiver.

Putting thought and planning into constructing a card and making it special is exceptionally satisfying. Inside this book, you will find everything that you need to know to get started on what can be an incredibly rewarding hobby.

Make stunning and stylish cards for men, women and children. Say congratulations, thank you and get well soon. For birthdays, easter, weddings, valentine's, christenings, new babies and general every days. This book will guide you through the materials and equipment that you need to make your own fantastic cards.

With step by step instructions to crafting pretty cards, we will take you through the process of getting started and inspire you to create your very own designs.

Instructions

Whether you've just started cardmaking or you're already a seasoned crafter, it's often worth taking a look at your 'life's essentials' and making sure you've got everything you're likely to need.

When you first start out cardmaking, it's a little like being let loose in a sweet shop. There will be the tendency to do a trolley dash in every hobby store and craft fair. Many people tend to regret a lot of their early buys, as their experience grows and they develop their own style and preferences. Many people do, however, agree on the card making basics, so this book highlights these along with some other card making 'life's essentials'.

Card making basics:

Adhesives: there's a mind-boggling array of adhesives on the market, but to start with your best bets are: double-sided tape, which can easily be trimmed to size; 3D foam tape or pads to add dimension; and a roller glue that is easy to dispense without making your fingers sticky.

Card: you can never have too much card! To give you flexibility in your designs, try making your own card blanks, as you can use just about any type and colour imaginable. A stash of white or cream card and envelopes are essential, and you will find 10 of each in this wallet.

Cardstock: you can never have too much card! Available in every shade imaginable and in different weights (thicknesses) to suit, cardstock is essential for matting, making your own card blanks, creating your own embellishments and much more.

Craft knife: there are many types of craft knives available and they prove indispensable when it comes to cutting and scoring. Invest in one that has a changeable blade, or a scalpel.

Cutting mat: you'll need two different types of cutting surface: a self-healing cutting mat for cutting, piercing and setting eyelets, and a PTFE-coated craft mat, preferably infused with glass for strength, non-stick and able to withstand high temperatures.

Decorative papers: there's much to be borrowed from scrapbooking, especially patterned paper, as so many are excellent for card backgrounds and offer good value for money coming in 12x12'' size.

Greetings: items such as rub-ons and peel-off greetings can be much maligned, but do serve a purpose, especially when you're stuck for a greeting in a hurry.

Heat gun: if you're going to be stamping and embossing, then this is an absolute essential. There are several designs to choose from, but it's a good idea to listen to other crafters' advice before you commit to a particular model.

Paper trimmer: essential for cutting pieces for layering and can help you to save money by cutting your own card blanks, as well as giving you the flexibility to make blanks from any sort of card to   co-ordinate with your designs.

Scoring board and bone folder: a bone folder to give you a nice finish to the card folds and a scoring board to get the proportions correct.

Scissors: a large pair of kitchen scissors is fine for non-precision, cutting, whereas you're likely to need a very small precision-tip pair for all the fiddly jobs that require pinpoint accuracy. You'll also be thankful for a pair of small Teflon-coated scissors to cut sticky materials with minimum hassle.

Things you might need:

Chalk inks: chalk inks are wonderful for creating backgrounds, just by sweeping across plain card. If you're not sure what you need, a number of inks are available in small sizes and can be the ideal low-cost choice for experimentation.

Craft knife and metal ruler: for cutting precision, particularly on shorter pieces and fiddly bits, these go well together. You should also avoid using wooden rulers.

Dies: metal dies are incredibly useful for cutting paper, cardstock and other materials into specific shapes. They come in a huge range of shapes and sizes, from simple squares and circles to ornate flowers and flourishes. While not an essential part of cardmaking they can make for much neater end results and are very handy when producing cards in bulk.

Embossing powders: you can choose coloured embossing powder with a clear ink, or you can choose a coloured ink with clear embossing powder. For best results with fine images, detail is the perfect choice.

Greetings messages: it's worth considering background patterns and a few designs that you can use as main focal images. Messages such as 'Happy Birthday', 'With Love', 'Thinking of You' and similar non gender-based messages will get plenty of use. For background images, a text panel, music and a pattern such as a mesh can be the mainstay of your growing collection. Alphabets are wonderful for spelling out messages, and can also be multi-stamped as backgrounds. For main images the world is your oyster, but be careful what you choose: florals and leaves, for example, are always a safe bet and can be mixed & matched and used continually, each time with a different look.

Inkpads: a potential minefield, so where do you start? If you're going to be stamping in your cardmaking projects, one of life's absolute essentials is a good black inkpad: one that gives you excellent coverage and is versatile enough for different card surfaces.

Manual die-cutting machine: in order to use dies to cut different materials you will need to purchase a die-cutting machine. The material you want to cut and the die you are using are placed between two cutting plates and fed through the machine. It works like a mangle, putting the plates under pressure in order to cut the die design into your material.

Off-the-shelf embellishments: very handy to have at hand for quick cardmaking. With so many on the market to choose from, try to pick ones that have a lot of appeal.

Pigment inks: generally, these are what you need if you're going to emboss, as they are slower drying than dye inks and allow you time to emboss.

Punches: hand punches are a cost-effective way of adding decorative main elements, as well as for corner and border decoration.

Rubber stamps: a stamper will probably argue that every rubberstamp in their collection is an essential item, but that's not exactly true! To avoid buying anything that simply looks nice, think about the types of cards that you're planning on making and consider the stamp designs that will be most useful to you.

Birthdays

Pretty Cupcake

You will need

- patterned paper & images
- brown card blank
- white cardstock
- stitched ribbon
- large scalloped circle punch
- white shrink plastic

Your step-by-step guide:

1 Cover the middle of the card blank with black & pink swirl-patterned paper and tie a length of ribbon around the card.

2 Print a cupcake image onto white cardstock and cut out. Add a doodled border with a black fineliner pen, and trim into a rectangle shape. Mount onto green patterned paper with foam pads and adhere to the card.

3 Create little embellishments from white shrink plastic using a scalloped punch. Add doodled details and make a hole in the centre of each one with an eyelet tool. Shrink according to the manufacturer's instructions using a heat gun or oven.

4 Attach each shrunk embellishment with a mini sprinkle brad as shown.

- mini sprinkle brads
- black permanent pen
- black fineliner pen
- foam pads
- double-sided tape
- eyelet tool

Three Windows

Your step-by-step guide:

1 Crease-fold white cardstock to create a 15x10 cm card blank. Attach pink cardstock to the inside of the card, then cut out three apertures from the front, the middle aperture measuring 50x35 mm and the two smaller apertures measuring 35x35 mm.

2 Punch two circles and handcut a rectangle from green cardstock. Draw dashes around each to create a border, then attach to the inside of the card behind the windows.

3 Stick acetate over the apertures, securing it inside the card. Stamp the bird and leaf images onto the acetate using permanent ink and colour using permanent pens.

4 Use the permanent pens to draw dashes around the windows, then complete the card by stamping or hand-writing the sentiment centrally.

You will need

- white cardstock
- green and pink cardstock
- acetate
- permanent coloured pens
- medium circle punch
- black inkpad
- bird stamp

So Sweet

Your step-by-step guide:

1. Stamp the bird design onto the bottom-right corner of the white card blank.

2. Trim a 10 mm strip of dotty paper to reveal one row of dots, and attach down the left-hand side of the card blank.

3. Cut cardstock into a 55 mm-wide strip and adhere to the left of the dotty strip.

4. Cut out a heart and bird design from patterned paper, and adhere to the paper strips as shown.

5. Draw a branch and leaves with a fineliner pen, and attach flowers and pearls to finish.

You will need

- clear bird stamps
- dotty paper
- cardstock
- white cardstock
- paper flowers
- self-adhesive pearls
- black fineliner pen

Butterfly Beauty

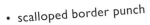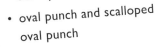

You will need

- pink and green cardstock
- patterned paper
- twine
- butterfly stamps
- turquoise and pink inkpads

- scalloped border punch
- oval punch and scalloped oval punch
- white cardstock
- glue gel

Your step-by-step guide:

1 Create a 10 cm-square card blank from pink cardstock and cover the front with green cardstock leaving a narrow pink border.

2 Cut a piece of patterned paper to 8.5 cm square and punch the bottom edge. Wrap twine around this piece and secure to the card front using glue gel.

3 Stamp a butterfly onto white cardstock using pink and turquoise inks.

4 Die-cut the image into an oval, then matt onto a scalloped oval die-cut from green cardstock using glue gel.

5 Attach the butterfly topper to the card front using glue gel.

Paper Flower

Your step-by-step guide:

1   Trim a piece of beige cardstock to fit across the centre of the card blank as shown.

2   Use the scalloped square die to create a pink scalloped edge and trim before attaching to the inside edge of your card front as shown.

3   Add a thin band of patterned paper and a length of ribbon tied into a bow to the front of the card.

4   Use a compass to draw three different-sized circles onto a combination of vellum, patterned and plain cardstock.

5   Fold each circle in half, in half again and then in half again. Unfold each one and lay them flat.

6   Using a craft knife and ruler make cuts between the fold lines from the edge of the circle to approximately 5 mm from the centre. When you have completed all three circular shapes, attach them together with PVA glue and fix into position on your card using a foam pad. Add a gem for decoration.

You will need

- blank papers and cardstock
- self-adhesive gem
- ribbon
- scalloped square die
- PVA glue

Vellum Flower

Your step-by-step guide:

1   Take a 4 cm strip of patterned paper and adhere it to the front of a square card blank approximately 3 cm from the bottom edge.

2   Use the scalloped circle die to create an aperture in the front of your card.

3   Trim a square from vellum to measure approximately 2 cm larger than the aperture, and affix it to the inside of the card using foam pads.

4   Die-cut several vellum flower shapes in different colours and use doublesided tape to fix them together, curling each flower petal as you do so and decorating the centre of the final layer with gems.

5   Attach the assembled flower into position in the centre of the aperture, using double-sided tape to secure.

You will need

- scalloped circle die
- flower die
- blank cardstock and paper
- patterned paper
- self-adhesive gems
- ribbon
- double sided tape

Pretty Butterflies

Your step-by-step guide:

1   Cut the background panel from the sheet of patterned paper and attach centrally to your card blank.

2   Remove all the internal background from the dragonfly peel-off images, using the tip of your craft knife to lift them.

3   Attach the dragonflies to orange paper and cut around them, starting at the base of the tail for ease and making sure you angle your scissors for undercutting.

4   Glue the dragonflies to your card blank using 3D foam pads to lift the wing tips. Repeat the process with duplicate images to create the pink wing layers then finish with a nailhead in the centre of each dragonfly.

You will need

- square card blank
- patterned papers
- dragonfly peel-offs
- nailheads
- 3D foam pads
- scissors
- craft knife

Stitched Up

Your step-by-step guide:

1 Trace and cut a flower from white felt.

2 Stitch around the inside of the flower using pink embroidery thread in a running stitch.

3 Draw a circle onto pink felt and cut it out. Cut a smaller circle from green felt and stick to the pink circle using double-sided tape.

4 Add a row of blanket stitch around the outside of the green circle.

5 Sew a green button to the centre of the circle and attach to the middle of the white flower.

6 Assemble layers of white felt and pink cardstock onto a dark green card blank before adding the white flower.

You will need

- white, pink and green felt
- embroidery thread
- needle
- button
- scissors
- double-sided tape
- green card blank

Ribbon Squares

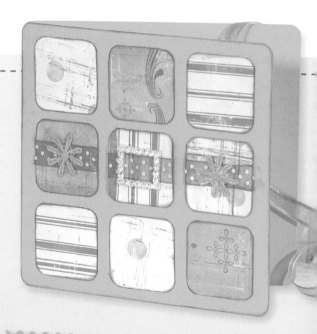

Your step-by-step guide:

1   Crease-fold a 30×15 cm piece of cardstock to create the base card, and round the corners.

2   Punch three squares each from three different patterned papers; round all the corners. Ink the edges of each square, as well as the card blank edges.

3   Stick the squares, evenly spaced, onto the card blank. Fix pieces of ribbon across each of the central three squares to create the illusion of weaving, adding a diamanté ribbon slide to the middle ribbon before attaching.

4   Cut two flowers from the braid and add over the ribbon to finish.

You will need

- cardstock
- square and corner-rounder punches
- floral braid
- ribbon slide
- polka dot ribbon
- patterned papers
- pink fluid chalk inkpad

Orchid

Your step-by-step guide:

1 Score an A4 sheet of card in half to make an A5 card blank.

2 Print out your backing paper and trim to 200x137 mm. Edge all four sides with a gold pen and attach to your base card using double-sided tape.

3 Mount your largest topper onto a 155x90 mm piece of gold mirri card using 3D foam tape, then affix to the centre of the card.

4 For extra depth, trim the inner section of another topper and attach over the original using 3D foam tape.

5 Découpage three orchids from an offcut of the backing paper, and attach to the bottom righthand corner of the topper using gel glue.

6 Wrap organza ribbon around the spine of the card, and tie into a bow to finish.

You will need

- gentle gloss photo paper
- card
- gold mirri card
- organza ribbon
- double-sided & 3D foam tape
- gold calligraphy pen
- gel glue
- découpage snips

Monster Birthday

Your step-by-step guide:

1 Sew twice around the edge of the card face using a straight stitch in orange thread.

2 To make the monster truck, punch one red 1 3/4" circle and cut in half. Cut one half into quarters. Attach one quarter underneath the half circle so you have a straight edge along the bottom of the truck. Adhere two black 1" circles and two silver 1/4" circles together and attach as wheels to the monster truck. Position the complete truck on the card using 3D foam pads.

3 To make the cars, punch 7/8" circles in blue and green cardstock and cut in half. Punch 1/2" circles from the same colours and cut these in half too. Adhere a smaller half under each larger semicircle. Punch the black wheels using a 1/4" circle punch and attach to the bottom of each car. Position the three cars in a row along the base of the card using double-sided tape.

4 Punch three yellow 1/2" circles and stick to a 6x1.5 cm strip of black cardstock to form a traffic light. Attach to the top right of the card.

5 Write or stamp your greeting along the top of the card above the monster truck.

You will need

- white card blank
- blue, yellow, red, black, silver and green cardstock
- orange thread
- black pen
- 1/4", 1/2", 7/8", 1" and 1 3/4" circle punches
- sewing machine
- 3D foam pads

Birthday Hugs

Your step-by-step guide:

1   Stamp the footballer image and colour with watercolour pencils remembering to add muddy patches. Stamp and colour the trophy, then trim around both.

2   Use a circular template to draw a 75 mm circle on the back of red gingham paper. Cut out and attach to the centre of a 12.5x12.5 cm card blank.

3   Draw zigzag faux stitching around the edges of the circle and stamp the greeting underneath.

4   Finish by attaching the footballer and trophy images to the circle using 3D foam pads.

You will need

- footballer and trophy stamp sets
- white cardstock
- red gingham paper
- watercolour pencils and waterbrush
- black fineline pen
- black inkpad
- 3D foam pads

Woodpecker

Your step-by-step guide:

1. Trim a piece of card to create your 8" square card blank.

2. Mount the woodpecker image onto white card then mount onto green card, trimming to leave a wide border.

3. Cut all the elements out of the remaining découpage sheets, and assemble onto the base image using gel glue.

4. Trim the patterned backing paper, mount onto green cardstock and trim to leave a narrow border, then attach to the base card.

5. Mount the woodpecker panel in the centre of the card using 3D foam tape, then wrap a piece of red organza ribbon around the spine to finish.

You will need

- various coloured cardstock
- double-sided tape
- foam tape
- gel glue
- red organza ribbon
- patterned paper
- woodpecker image

Power Sphere

Your step-by-step guide:

1 Create a 20x8cm card blank from white cardstock.

2 Using the template, cut the cylindrical part of the machine from green cardstock, and the base, rings and sphere band from silver cardstock. Ink the edges using a black inkpad, then use a blending pad to add white highlights down the cylinder.

3 Use a 2.5cm circle die to cut the sphere from copper cardstock, then ink the edges using a brown inkpad.

4 Attach the sphere to the card blank and trim the overlapping edge. Attach the dark green cylinder shape, the silver base and rings. Trim the card blank to fit, as shown.

5 Draw a bolt of lightning onto the sphere band using a glue pen. Allow to dry slightly before adding copper leaf. Once dry, gently brush away any excess copper leaf.

6 Punch two circles from coloured cardstock and fix together with a screw brad. Attach to the sphere band to finish.

Cheers!

Your step-by-step guide:

1. Cover a 12.5 cm-square card blank with patterned paper. Matt a 3.5 cm strip of striped paper with dark brown paper, and trim to leave a narrow border. Attach across the centre of the card.

2. Stamp your digi image onto white cardstock, colour using watercolour pencils and die-cut into a circle.

3. Layer the image circle onto a 10 cm square of polka dot-patterned paper, and attach to the centre of the card using 3D foam pads.

4. Decorate the corners of the polka dot square using aqua rainbow drops to finish.

You will need

- patterned papers
- digi stamps
- chalk ink
- rainbow drops
- watercolour pencils
- white cardstock
- circle dies

Gone Fishing

Your step-by-step guide:

1 Trim a piece of patterned paper to fit the front of a 14.5 cm-square card blank, leaving a narrow border around the edges.

2 Cut a 9.5x11.5 cm piece of polka dot-patterned paper and adhere towards the left-hand side of the card. Decorate with a strip of co-ordinating patterned paper as shown.

3 Stamp your digi image onto white cardstock, colour using watercolour pencils and trim into a rectangle. Matt with cream patterned paper and ink the edges. Add two patterned paper tabs to the lower right-hand corner of the panel and decorate with card candy.

4 Attach the finished image panel to the centre of the card using 3D foam pads.

You will need

- patterned paper
- digi stamps
- card candy
- watercolour pencils
- white cardstock
- chalk ink

Shaker Card

Your step-by-step guide:

1   Using the die with the magnetic flower shape positioned in the bottom corner, create your yellow colour core card blank.

2   Stick a piece of acetate to the inside of the card to cover the aperture you have created. Use a double layer of foam pads to create a wall around the aperture shape on the inside of the card, ensuring there are no spaces between the foam pads.

3   Put small seed beads inside the wall of foam pads and cover with a piece of orange card.

4   Turn the card over and attach a piece of patterned paper to cover half of the front, then decorate with a length of knotted ribbon held with double-sided tape.

Birthday Wishes

Your step-by-step guide:

1 Stamp the gingham image onto the card front using black ink.

2 Stamp the same image onto white cardstock using purple and blue ink.

3 Cut two purple and two blue 2.5 cm squares from these pieces and matt onto purple cardstock using 3D foam pads. Secure to the card front as shown.

4 Write your birthday words onto white cardstock using black ink and cut out one of the sentiments. Matt onto purple cardstock using 3D foam pads, then affix below the stamped squares to complete your design.

You will need

- gingham stamp
- acrylic block
- white 13.5 cm-square card blank
- white & purple cardstock
- purple, blue and black inkpads
- sticky tape
- 3D foam pads

Comms Tower

Your step-by-step guide:

1   Create an A6 card blank from pearlescent copper cardstock and line the inside surface with silver cardstock. Ink the edges of the copper cardstock using a brown inkpad and the silver cardstock using a brown inkpad. Use blending pads to soften.

2   Draw a cone shape onto yellow-gold cardstock and cut out. Cut narrow strips of dark green cardstock and attach them to the yellow-gold cone using the lines as a guide. Attach the crossed lines first, then the longer, vertical strips. Use a pen nib to add brown ink to the outside edges of the diamond shapes created by the dark green card strips. Attach the tower to the card front.

3   Cut out the tower base and rings from charcoal cardstock and attach. Add two small circles and a pointed tip to the top of the tower.

4   Trim the card front to fit the right-hand edge of the tower so that the silver interior of the card is visible.

5   Punch a series of circles from yellow-gold cardstock, ink the edges using a brown inkpad and affix to the left-hand side of the card front.

You will need

- copper, yellow-gold, silver, dark green and charcoal pearlescent cardstock
- black fluid chalk inkpad
- brown pigment inkpad
- blending foam pads
- pen nibs
- 0.5 cm, 0.8 cm, I cm, 1.2 cm, 1.8 cm, 2.5 cm circle punches

Cupcake Stack

Your step-by-step guide:

1 Sew twice around the edge of the card front using a straight stitch in yellow thread.

2 Punch three pink and three grey 1½" circles from coloured cardstock.

3 Use deckled-edged scissors to trim the pink circles and decorate each using 1/4" circles of blue, green and yellow cardstock.

4 Carefully remove 5 mm on a slight angle from the two sides of each grey circle to form the cupcake case bases. Draw a scalloped line along the base and straight lines up from each scallop.

5 Attach the grey bases to the card front and adhere the pink icing to the top of each grey circle using 3D foam pads. Decorate the top of each cupcake with a pink paper flower and pearl centre.

6 Tie a bow from pink gingham ribbon and position under the cupcakes, then write or stamp a sentiment under the design to finish.

You will need

- white card blank
- pink, grey, blue, yellow and green cardstock
- pink paper flowers
- pink gingham ribbon
- yellow thread
- cream self-adhesive pearls
- 1/4" and 1 1/2" circle punches
- sewing machine
- deckle-edged scissors

Mice

Your step-by-step guide:

1   Sew twice around the edge of the card front using a straight stitch in light blue thread.

2   Attach ribbon across the card, around 3 cm from the bottom edge.

3   To make the large mouse, punch a 1¾" circle from grey cardstock and trim the base. Add two pink ¾" circles as ears and attach to the card using 3D foam pads. Glue on two goggle eyes and a black pearl for the nose. Draw in whiskers, tail and ear definitions using a black pen.

4   For the smaller mice, punch two grey 1" circles and four pink ½" circles. Trim the bases from the two grey circles, one nearly in half. Attach the pink circles as ears, making sure one ear on each mouse sits behind the grey circle.

5   Decorate the smaller mice with goggle eyes, whiskers, tails and a pearl nose before attaching to the card using foam pads.

6   Write or stamp the sentiment under the ribbon to complete your card.

You will need

- white card blank
- pink and grey cardstock
- goggle eyes
- pink spotted ribbon
- light blue thread

- black self-adhesive pearls
- black pen
- ½", ¾", 1", 1½" and 1¾" circle punches
- sewing machine

Ladybugs

Your step-by-step guide:

1. Sew twice around the edge of the card front using red thread, once using a straight stitch and then with a wide zigzag stitch.

2. Punch two red and two black 1" circles. Cut the red circles in half and glue on top of the black circles with the top tips overlapping, creating wings. Add three black pearls to each wing.

3. Punch two 1/2" black circles and stick under the 1" black circles where the red tips meet, forming the bugs' heads.

4. Position the green flowers along the base of the card and add a green button to the centre of each one.

5. Place the completed ladybugs onto the card using 3D foam pads and add a sentiment in the top righthand corner.

You will need

- white card blank
- black and red cardstock
- light green flowers
- green buttons

- black self-adhesive pearls
- red thread
- black pen
- 1/2" and 1" circle punches
- sewing machine

Toadstool House

Your step-by-step guide:

1. Sew twice around the edge of the card face using a straight stitch in light blue thread.

2. To make the toadstool, punch a red 1¾" circle and trim the base. Affix three white ½" circles on top. Punch a yellow 1" circle and attach to the card using tape. Place the head of the toadstool above this using 3D foam pads.

3. To make the flower, punch one white and five blue ¾" circles. Position the blue circles so they overlap one another around the white circle. Decorate the centre of the flower using three yellow self-adhesive pearls.

4. Attach the flower to the card using 3D foam tape and draw a stem in black pen. Cut a green ¾" circle in half to make two leaves and affix on opposite sides of the stem.

5. Punch small green circles using the ¼" and 1/16" punches and attach under the toadstool. Draw tiny stems using a black pen.

6. Write or stamp a sentiment at the top of the card to finish

Cowboy

Your step-by-step guide:

1   Cut out the horseshoe, riding cowboy and three stars from the template.

2   Trim two rectangular mounts from dark brown cardstock, one approximately 4 cm shorter than the other. Matt and layer a variety of patterned paper from the stack onto the mounts as shown.

3   Spray the riding cowboy with spray gloss to create a glossy effect, and fix to the smaller rectangular mount using 3D foam pads. Arrange the panels onto the front of an orange 8 cm square card blank.

4   To make the cowboy, follow the instructions provided in the pack to assemble.

5   Assemble, then mount onto the right-hand panel of the card before adding peel-offs and facial details to finish.

You will need

- 8" square card blank
- cowboy theme template
- pale pink cardstock
- glue
- paper stack
- brown cardstock
- varnish spray gloss
- clear self-adhesive gemstones
- peel-offs
- 3D foam pads

Pretty Flowers

Your step-by-step guide:

1. Stamp four mini buttons onto lilac cardstock using an embossing inkpad. Coat with embossing powder, tap off the excess and heat. Once cool, cut out the buttons and leave to one side.

2. Trim a 14×28 cm piece of cream cardstock, and fold in half to create a 14 cm - square base card.

3. Using an online card library, print out your chosen frame to measure 12.5 cm square, along with your chosen character image. Matt the frame with lilac cardstock using narrow shaker tape, leaving a 2 mm border on each edge. Mount onto the card front.

4. Decorate the frame as required using a glue pen and crystal glitter. Use narrow shaker tape to attach your character image to the frame.

5. Print a sheet of purple flowers from the online library and follow the instructions to create three floral embellishments with the petal punches. Attach to the bottom-left of the frame. Add a mini button to each corner of the frame to finish.

You will need

- embellishment stamps
- embossing inkpad
- embossing powder
- heat gun
- lilac and cream cardstock

- super-smooth paper
- glue pen
- crystal glitter
- petal punches

Blast Off!

Your step-by-step guide:

1. Cover the front of a tall, thin card blank with blue cardstock and ink the edges. Use the template on the right to cut the slider panel from blue cardstock and ink the edges.

2. Cut a 4.5x3 cm strip of blue cardstock. Hold this behind the aperture you have cut in the slider panel and attach foam pads along the full length and width of the aperture so that it fits in place and will only slide up and down. Adhere the aperture panel to the card blank using double-sided tape only around the edges, keeping the foam-padded slider in place. Ensure that the slider still moves up and down freely.

3. Stamp numbers down the left-hand side of the card and add black pen dots.

4. Use the template to cut flames from yellow cardstock. Use inkpads to add colour to the flames and affix in place. Use the red inkpad to colour the area of blue card visible through the aperture between the flames.

5. Use the template to cut the rocket pieces from cardstock and ink the edges of each piece using charcoal ink. Assemble the rocket and check the position of the rocket at the bottom and top of the slider before attaching. Affix it to the foam pads on the slider – the foam pads should be placed in the centre of the rocket between the two stripes for the slide and reveal effect to work properly. Add white pen highlights to finish.

You will need

- blue red, yellow and pearlescent white and silver cardstock
- charcoal, red, blue, black and light and dark orange inkpads
- black felt pen
- white gel pen
- number stamps
- yellow vellum
- templates
- circle punches

Greeting Cards

Thank You

Your step-by-step guide:

1   Create a 5x4" card blank and cover with patterned paper then ink the edges.

2   Stamp the image onto acetate and run through a sticker maker. Peel away the backing sheet, apply glitter and press down gently. Shake off the excess glitter and trim.

3   Attach the image glitter-side down onto the card with a small amount of glue and add the sticky jewel accent.

4   Write your sentiment onto white cardstock, ink the edges and layer onto a small strip of yellow cardstock. Attach to the bottom of the card with foam tape.

You will need

- green, white and yellow cardstock
- patterned paper
- angel stamp
- acetate
- red inkpad
- brown inkpad
- heart sticky jewel
- pink ultra-fine glitter

So Nice of You

Your step-by-step guide:

1. Stamp and emboss the single daisy rectangle three times. Watercolour using the brush markers and cut out.

2. Cut three 2.5x3.7 cm pieces of pink card and use the pink inkpad to sponge the edges. Mount the stamped images onto these using foam pads, and layer each onto pink paisley paper.

3. Stick the flowers across the card as shown, and finish with your written sentiment below.

You will need

- square card blank
- daisy stamp set
- paisley papers
- pink cardstock
- brush markers
- pink inkpad

Birds of a Feather

Your step-by-step guide:

1. Cut patterned paper to 95x80 mm and attach to the bottom half of white card stock.

2. Stamp the bird image onto the card, starting from the bottom left-hand corner.

3. Trim your cardstock into a 10 mm strip and edge with the border punch. Affix down the left-hand side of the card blank.

4. Attach paper and lace flowers to the card, then embellish with self-adhesive pearls to finish.

You will need

- clear bird stamps
- a variety of cardstock
- 20 mm, 35 mm and 50 mm flowers

- border punch
- lace daisies
- black self-adhesive pearls
- patterned paper

Doily Vase

Your step-by-step guide:

1. Emboss a sheet of patterned paper using an embossing folder. Match up the embossed pattern on the remaining paper and run through the machine again.

2. Create a background paper by stamping within the diamonds using the stamp with green ink, the leaf stamp with dark green and the ribbon swirl with blue. Ink the stamp each time, before stamping. When dry, cut out the embossed and patterned part of the paper and affix to the front of a white 14 cm-square card blank. Because of the size of the embossing folder, it will fall short of the card spine, so use the doily punch to punch an edge in a contrasting patterned paper (save the waste strip), then in the same paper to cover the space. Finish with the waste strip from the contrasting paper.

3. Die-cut a circle from smooth white cardstock and stamp the vase stamp using blue ink. Add in and ink. Rotate the stamps and stamp at least twice before reinking. Add sprig stamp in dark green ink and leaf stamp in green, turning the placement line towards the flowers. Add ribbon swirl stamp in blue ink.

4. Ink the edges of the circle using yellow chalk or ink, then matt onto a scalloped circle die-cut from patterned paper then onto a doily. Affix to the card front.

5. Die-cut two dragonflies from cream cardstock and attach to the card front using 3D foam pads. Decorate with yellow pearls and glitter glue to finish.

You will need

- white 14 cm square blank card
- white and cream cardstock
- patterned paper
- flower rubber stamp
- yellow pearls
- various coloured inkpads
- flower, sprig, leaf and vase rubber stamps
- yellow chalk
- doily punch
- embossing folder
- dragonfly cutting die
- die cutting machine
- circle die cutter
- 3D foam pads
- glitter glue

Floral Fan

Your step-by-step guide:

1. Take four yellow flowers and three pink flowers and twist the stems together. Wrap the flowers and fans together using organza ribbon.

2. Cover the card front with patterned paper, then add a 3.5x14.5 cm strip of navy cardstock to the righthand side and add a piece of organza ribbon on top.

3. Cut the stem off one of the flowers and twist round the outside of the organza ribbon, leaving excess at the back of the bunch, then carefully pierce a hole approximately a third of the way up the card front. Thread the excess stem through and secure using double-sided tape.

You will need

- cream 10x14.5 cm card blank
- navy blue cardstock
- A4 paper
- yellow organza ribbon
- pink & yellow art flowers
- white with silver trim art fans
- gold inkpad

Pretty Beads

Your step-by-step guide:

1. Sponge one ink of your choice onto one side of a domino-sized piece of stampboard and a different coloured ink onto the other side. Stamp over the piece with a texture block using your first choice of ink.

2. Let the whole thing dry completely, then pat the inkpad over the surface. Cover with enamel and heat to melt. Repeat three times to build up a thick layer of enamel.

3. Fix a ball of sticky-tack onto the underside of the piece and use it to steady the surface of the stampboard while you add gold dry glitter around the edge of the stampboard and on the circles on the design, then leave to dry.

4. Cut a small piece of beaded trim and fix it to the back of the stampboard using tape. Attach the pin fastener.

5. Assemble the flower elements together and stick to the front of the stampboard.

- gold glitter glue
- craft flowers
- small rosebud
- beaded trim
- sticky tack
- stamp set
- self-adhesive pin back

You will need

- stampboard
- a variety of inkpads
- watermark inkpad
- embossing enamel

Congratulations

Your step-by-step guide:

1. Crease-fold a piece of 4x5 1/2" maroon cardstock to form the card base.

2. Ink up a swirl stamp with ink and stamp onto the tea towel fabric.

3. Cut the stamped image out and fray the edges by snipping with the very tip of a pair of scissors.

4. Attach the fabric piece to the front of the card and add a machine-stitched border using light blue thread.

5. Decorate with a paper flower and brad, then add your hand written greeting and affix.

You will need

- star die
- die-cutting machine
- paper pack
- glitter gems
- blue and brown cardstock
- brown inkpad
- glitter glue

Christmas Cards

The Gift of Christmas

Your step-by-step guide:

1   Cut a square of mid-blue cardstock to fit the card front, distress the edges, then attach.

2   Print out the green snowflake paper and distress then ink the edges. Matt with green cardstock, distress the edges again, and fix to the centre of the card.

3   Stamp the gift stack onto white cardstock, and colour using watercolour crayons and a waterbrush. Trim to measure 7.5x5.5 cm, then distress and ink the edges.

4   Cut an oblong of blue cardstock to measure 8x6 cm and an oblong of green cardstock to 9x7 cm. Round the corners and distress the edges, then layer and attach to the card. Mount the stamped image on top using 3D foam pads.

4   Tie polka dot ribbon around the spine of the card and knot at the front. Highlight with glitter glue and add three self-adhesive pearls to the bottom-right corner.

You will need

- stamp pad foam
- white 5"-square card blank
- white cardstock
- corner-rounder punch
- black inkpad
- polka dot ribbon

- glitter glue
- green and red self-adhesive pearls
- water colour crayons
- blue and green cardstock
- distressing tool
- distress inkpad

Starbright

Your step-by-step guide:

1 Create four white clay stars by applying a cutter to a sheet of white modelling clay. Bake the clay following the manufacturer's instructions and allow it to cool.

2 Layer the card blank with panels of green, red and white paper.

3 Cut a 10 cm-tall triangular tree from a piece of green cardstock and a narrow 4 cm pot from red cardstock.

4 Insert brads at equal intervals to the inner edges of the tree, and fix both the tree and the pot to the card using 3D foam pads.

5 Attach the clay stars to the card.

You will need

- white modelling clay
- white A6 card blank
- star cutter set
- green, red and white paper and cardstock
- tiny green and red brads
- non-stick roller, PVA glue, sticky foam pads
- baking surface and domestic oven

Christmas Trees

Your step-by-step guide:

1   Cut out three triangles (4 cm wide and 6 cm tall)
    from the lime green cardstock. Attach strips of
    double-sided tape diagonally across each. Remove the
    backing from the tape, and sprinkle with gold glitter.
    Tap off the excess.

2   Cut a 13x8.5 cm piece of pale yellow cardstock.
    Punch three stars from yellow cardstock, and mount
    onto the pale yellow panel along with the three trees,
    using foam pads. Add rhinestones.

3   Matt your tree panel with lime green cardstock
    leaving a narrow border.

4   Fold an A5 piece of yellow cardstock
    in half to form your card blank.
    Apply a strip of glitter across the
    middle using the same technique as
    above, then affix the tree panel onto
    the front.

You will need

- star punch
- red, green and yellow 4 mm
  self-adhesive rhinestones
- gold ultra-fine glitter
- pale yellow, golden yellow
  and lime green cardstock
- 6 mm double-sided tape
- double-sided foam tape

Snowy Day

Your step-by-step guide:

1   Crease-fold white cardstock to create a 15 cm-square card blank. Trim scroll paper to fit and matt with purple then silver cardstock. Wrap with lilac ribbon and attach to the card front.

2   Stamp the your chosen image with black ink. Colour with a variety of markers and then sprinkle with ultra thick embossing powder. Heat with a heat gun.

3   Once the embossing powder has melted, repeat this step twice more. Allow to cool, then cut into a circle shape and matt with purple cardstock.

4   Use a die cutting machine and snowflake die to cut a snowflake from white glitter card and attach to the top of the card front, overlapping the ribbon.

5   Mount your embossed image in the centre of the card, slightly overlapping the snowflake. Make a bow from a small piece of lilac ribbon and adhere to the top of the image.

6   Punch three small snowflakes from purple and silver cardstock and white glitter card using a snowflake punch. Affix in the bottom-right of the card, fixing silver stones to the centre of each to finish.

You will need

- an image of your choice
- white, silver and purple card stock
- scroll paper
- snowflake stamp
- lilac ribbon

- silver gemstones
- black inkpad
- watermark inkpad
- embossing powder
- heat gun
- embossing machine
- snowflake die
- snowflake punch

Pretty Poinsettia

Your step-by-step guide:

1   Fix the entire design sheet onto white cardstock and cut out all the elements.

2   Ink the edges of a 5x7" card blank with fluid chalk ink. Print and trim a sheet of harlequin-patterned paper to slightly smaller than the card blank, and fix into position.

3   Print and trim checked paper to sit in the centre of the harlequin paper and fix into position again.

4   Rub gold fluid ink lightly over a white tag and thread with cream rickrack. Fix to the centre of the card blank, at an angle.

5   Curl the petals and layer them together, then push a jumbo brad through the centre to secure. Bend the spine of each of the leaves and fix to the back of the flower using gloss medium.

6   Ensuring there is sufficient gloss medium on the back of the flower, fix to the centre of the tag. Stick the flower centre over the jumbo brad, then cover the different sections with gold glitter glue.

You will need

- poinsettia design sheet
- white tag
- cream rickrack
- gold fluid chalk inkpad
- gold glitter glue
- white cardstock
- jumbo brad
- gloss medium
- harlequin-patterned paper

Christmas Penguin

Your step-by-step guide:

1   Trim a 13x5 cm strip of striped paper and adhere across the bottom of a 14x10 cm kraft card blank.

2   Print out your penguin image, trim into a circle shape and colour using watercolour pencils, then highlight using PVA glue and ultra-fine glitter.

3   Matt your image with a circle of blue paper and attach to the top lefthand corner of your card blank.

4   Take a 2.5 cm-wide strip of patterned paper and zigzag fold. Glue the ends together to create a flower and add a brad to the centre. Affix to the bottom right-hand corner of your card.

You will need

- Christmas paper pad
- stamp template
- penguin image
- kraft card blank
- white cardstock
- watercolour aquabrush
- PVA glue
- glitter

Christmas Tag

Your step-by-step guide:

1   Cut two patterned paper matts to fit the card front and attach together. Stamp snowflakes in the top-left and bottom-right corners and heat-emboss.

2   Cut a tag shape from cardstock, emboss using the embossing folder, distress the edges then matt onto a slightly larger patterned paper tag.

3   Set an eyelet in the top of the tag, thread ribbon through then secure to the card front at an angle using silicone glue.

4   Die-cut the village image from patterned paper and, with the die-cut still in the die, brush water mark over the rooftops. Remove the die-cut from the die, sprinkle with embossing powder and heat.

5   Place the die-cut back into the die and brush turquoise ink over the tree. Remove the die-cut, edge with sepia ink then attach to the tag using 3D foam pads. Add glitter glue to the edges of the tag to finish.

You will need

- cream 10.5x14.8 cm card blank
- patterned paper
- cardstock
- snowflakes stamps
- white embossing powder
- watermark inkpad
- heat tool

- embossing folder
- die-cutting machine
- turquoise & sepia inkpads
- squeeze tool
- glitter glue
- eyelet
- sheer ribbon
- silicone glue & 3D foam pads

Snow Fun

Your step-by-step guide:

1. Create an A6 card blank from watercolour paper. Use tracing paper to transfer the houses template to the inside surface. Draw over the image using permanent ink.

2. Transfer the background line only of the snowmen template onto the card front. Cut around the edges of both pictures to form a shaped card blank.

3. Transfer the snowmen section onto watercolour paper along with the two separate banks of snow from the houses template. Draw over the pictures with ink, rub away the pencil line and cut out.

4. Add watercolour crayon to the areas shown and blend with a brush. Add patches of blue crayon to the snowy areas to create shadow.

5. Attach the snowmen panel and banks of snow to the front of the card with foam pads. Add glitter glue swirls to the snowy areas to finish.

You will need

- watercolour paper (90gsm)
- tracing paper
- watercolour crayons
- watercolour brush
- glitter glue
- black permanent pen
- blue chalk
- template (below)

Easter
Cards

Easter Eggs

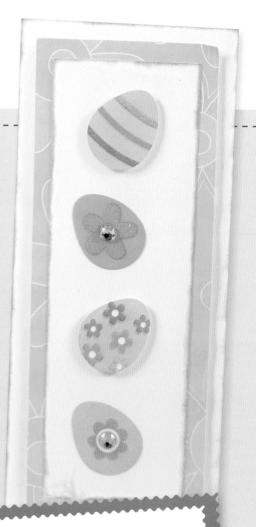

Your step-by-step guide:

1. Cut 2" from the open side of your card blank so that it now measures 3x7". Direct ink the edges using green fluid chalk.

2. Using one of the offcuts, cut 1" from the top. Direct ink the edges in green fluid chalk, then matt onto the pink patterned paper. Crop to form a ½" border all round. Matt centrally onto the card blank using 3D foam pads.

3. Choose four of the decorated eggs from the sticker sheet and fix onto the panel, adhering the first and third eggs with foam pads to raise them from the card.

4. As a finishing touch and to add some bling, fix an adhesive gem to the centre of the second and fourth eggs.

You will need

- easter sticker sheet
- craft essentials kit
- white 5x7" card blank
- green fluid chalk inkpad
- double-sided tape
- 3D foam pads

Pretty Circles

Your step-by-step guide:

1   Make an A6-sized side-fold card blank from cardstock, and trim 1 cm off the front righthand edge. Punch four 1 1/2" circles from the patterned papers and attach down the right-hand side of the card, making sure you line them up with the back edge.

2   Punch a 3" circle from green cardstock and a 2 1/2" circle from cream cardstock. Stamp and emboss your image onto the smaller circle and colour with water colour. Layer the circles together and attach to the card base using 3D foam pads.

3   Cut out a small daisy from the patterned paper, attach to the card, and add candy buttons down the right-hand side of the card and in the centre of the flower.

You will need

- 1 1/2", 3" and 2 1/2" circle punches
- daisy shapecut
- watercolour set
- variety of patterned papers
- varity of cardstock
- candy buttons
- image stamp

Easter Bonnet

Your step-by-step guide:

1   Make a 14.4 cm-square tent-fold card blank from cardstock.

2   Trim a piece of patterned paper to 14.4x7.5 cm and attach across the bottom of the card. Cover the join with a craft frill.

3   Cut cardstock to 9 cm square, and tape ribbon tabs to the top right-hand edge.

4   Stamp and emboss your image onto an 8.5 cm square of cardstock, and colour using watercolour set. Attach to the panel and attach to the centre of the card, then add candy buttons.

You will need

- watercolour set
- striped paper
- craft frill
- variety of cardstock
- yellow ribbon
- candy buttons

Hey Chick!

Your step-by-step guide:

1   Make a 14.4 cm-square side-fold card blank from cream cardstock.

2   Trim the patterned papers to measure 12x12.5 cm. Hold together with a paper clip whilst you cut a wavy edge along the top, then cut into three 4 cm strips. Matt with green cardstock, leaving a narrow border, and trim to follow the curve along the top. Attach to the centre of the card.

3   Cut a strip of green cardstock and stick to the righthand side of the card, then fix two buttons to the right-hand edge.

3   Stamp and emboss your image onto a 7x5 cm piece of cream cardstock, then colour using watercolour set. Matt with green cardstock, leaving a narrow border around the edges, and attach to the card using 3D foam pads.

You will need

- watercolour set
- patterned papers
- cream and green cardstock
- pastel buttons

Wedding
Cards

Sweet Matrimony

Your step-by-step guide:

1 Fold a piece of 28x14 cm white cardstock to make a square card blank. Ink the edges with the pink inkpad.

2 Dab the edges of 13.5x13.5 cm blue card with a water mark inkpad and randomly stamp with the hearts. Affix to the card blank using double-sided tape.

3 Stamp with cake stamp black ink onto white card measuring 7.1x7.6 cm. Stamp a second time onto matching cardstock and cut out the bow and heart.

4 Ink the edges of the stamped piece in pink, and layer onto blue and lilac card using double-sided tape. Matt again onto white card, edged in the same way.

5 Affix the matted image, bow and heart to the card blank using foam pads.

6 Finish by colouring in the stamped image with water colour pens using the watercolour paint technique.

You will need

- black inkpad
- pink inkpad
- water colour stamp pad
- cake stamp
- water colour pens
- paintbrush
- acrylic block
- white, blue, and lilac cardstock

Wedding Wishes

You will need

- groom and bride images
- white cardstock
- silver mirri card
- gemstones
- black ribbon

- scalloped and straight rectangles & scalloped and straight oval dies
- embossing folder
- die-cutting machine
- pc & printer
- foam pads

Your step-by-step guide:

1. Create a 10x21 cm card blank from white cardstock.

2. Cut a heart shape from silver mirri card.

3. Cut a piece of white ribbon to measure approximately 20 cm long and glue the dress stand to the centre, then affix to the card front.

4. Emboss the dress and groom, adhere both and decorate with gemstones.

5. Cut the ends of the ribbon to form a fringed effect, fold to form a shoulder wrap effect and glue down. Add gems to finish.

Silver Heart Wedding

Your step-by-step guide:

1. Stamp the bride & groom image onto white cardstock. Allow to dry, then colour using marker pens and trim.

2. Die-cut a large heart from silver cardstock, and mount the bride & groom onto the heart using 3D foam pads. Punch tiny hearts from mid-blue cardstock and attach, then decorate the bride with pearls.

3. Cut a piece of navy cardstock to 11x12.5 cm and round the corners. Stick a strip of 10x12 cm patterned paper across the panel, then mount the silver heart in the centre.

4. Trim a 7 cm-wide section from the front panel of the card front, and round the edges. Attach the image panel as shown, affixing only on the left-hand side.

5. Tie ribbon into a knot around the left-hand side of the card, and add glitter glue highlights to finish.

You will need

- black inkpad
- marker pens
- white 14.5 cm-square card blank
- white, mid-blue, royal blue and silver cardstock
- flat-backed pearls

- white sheer polka dot ribbon
- glitter glue
- corner-rounder punch
- heart border punch
- heart die
- various patterned papers
- wedding stamps

Wedding Day Invite

Your step-by-step guide:

1. Cut the 12x12" pearlised cardstock in half, then score and fold at 7.5 cm and 21 cm.

2. Stamp the butterfly and a swirl onto the front of the card.

3. Cut 12" pieces of dusty pink and sage ribbon, layer together and thread on a diamanté buckle. Wrap around the top panel of the card and secure on the reverse.

4. Add gemstones to the stamped images.

5. Matt pieces of cream pearlised cardstock onto dusty pink and lightgreen pearlised cardstock to fit into the pocket. Add gemstones to finish.

You will need

- cream 12x12" pearlised cardstock
- light green and dusty pink A4 pearlised
- cardstock white pearlised paper
- dusty pink 2.5 mm ribbon
- sage 15 mm organza ribbon
- square diamante buckle
- dark pink inkpad
- butterfly and swirl stamp set
- silver gems

Wedding Cheer

Your step-by-step guide:

1. Crease-fold a piece of cardstock to create your card blank.

2. Cut a panel of cardstock, cover with first choice of patterned papers, ink and stitch around the edge.

3. Attach the lace, tie on the twine and fix the panel to the card front.

4. Die-cut shapes from kraft cardstock and choice of patterned paper and adhere to the card front.

5. Colour seam binding using your marker pens, tie in a bow, add a button and adhere to the card. Add flowers below the bow.

6. Apply the rub-on to a piece of cardstock, die-cut, tie with twine and adhere to the card front to finish.

You will need

- various cardstock
- complimentary patterned paper
- lace, button, twine and seam binding
- foam and paper flowers

- pearl button
- brown chalk inkpad
- a choice of rub-on marker pens
- manual die-cutting machine
- die templates
- needle and thread

Easel Card

Your step-by-step guide:

1 Score, fold and trim white cardstock to create a 15 cm square card blank. Score one half of the card in half again and fold inwards. Apply strong tape to the bottom quarter of the folded card bank. Trim a 15 cm square of white cardstock and adhere to the card base.

2 Cut two 14.2 cm squares of patterned paper, ink the edges using distress ink and adhere to two slightly larger pieces of kraft cardstock. Stitch around the edges of the squares. Punch two strips of kraft cardstock and trim to measure 6 cm x the width of the base paper. Affix in place, adhere lace and seam binding ribbon across the front and base layers as shown, and fix a bow over this using strong wet glue to secure the charm. Attach this to the card front.

3 Stamp or print your sentiment, ink the edges using distress inkpad and adhere to kraft cardstock. Stitch around the edges of the paper and fix on the base of easel card using 3D foam pads.

4 Stamp the wedding background and bridal couple stamps and colour using marker pens. Trim the background image to a rectangle, ink the edges using distress ink and matt onto kraft cardstock. Stitch around the edges of the paper. Cut out the couple, apply glitter glue to the flowers and the bride's dress and then adhere the couple in place using 3D foam pads.

5 Punch leaves and fix in place on the card front together with the flowers, pearl pins and selfadhesive pearl hearts.

6 Stamp or print your sentiment, cut into a banner shape and fix in place on the card.

You will need

- blue and green paper pad
- white and kraft cardstock
- wedding background
- bridal couple stamps
- border punch
- leaf punch
- seam binding ribbon
- lace

- paper flower mulberries
- pearl pins
- self-adhesive pearl hearts
- distress inkpad
- charm
- glitter glue
- needle and thread
- 3D foam pads

New Baby!

Tiny Toes

Your step-by-step guide:

1 Create a 4"-square card blank from pink cardstock. Cover the bottom half of the card with patterned paper.

2 Draw an 'X' in the centre of the card front, with the outermost points where you want the corners of your opening to be. Cut along these lines with a craft knife to give four triangular flaps. Rip these triangles out, curling and scuffing the edges as you go.

3 Glue a piece of ribbon across the front of the card, over the paper join and across the aperture. Tie the tag around the top of the card with the same ribbon, and finish with a crystal gem.

You will need

- patterned cardstock
- paper
- a variety of ribbons
- chipboard tag
- crystal gem

Bouncy Baby

Your step-by-step guide:

1 Colour in your rabbit die-cut and highlight with glitter glue. Set aside to dry, before attaching to the card front.

2 Stamp the letters onto the foampad using a permanent inkpad. Attach to the card front using foam pad.

3 Wrap ribbon around the card front and tie to secure.

You will need

- 96 mm-square scalloped card blank
- rabbit die-cut
- 3D foam pads
- ribbon
- glitter glue
- alphabet stamps
- permanent black inkpad

New Baby

Your step-by-step guide:

1 Cover the front of an A6 card blank with patterned paper. Cut a 5 cm-wide strip of white cardstock using scallopedged scissors and attach across the card front. Cut a 3 cm strip of yellow cardstock and attach to the white strip.

2 Add faux stitching to the yellow strip using an orange felt-tip pen.

3 Cut an 8.5 cm square of turquoise cardstock and a 7x8 cm rectangle of white cardstock. Attach the white rectangle to the turquoise square using a strip of double-sided tape at the centre only. Pierce a series of holes through the two layers by following the template. Secure the embroidery thread to the back of the cardstock and use the template to follow the stitching pattern along both edges of the cardstock pieces. Fix to the card front.

4 Use the template to cut two booties from yellow cardstock. Colour the edges of each with yellow ink and draw faux stitching lines using an orange pen. Cut two narrow strips of white cardstock using scallop-edged scissors and attach to the top of each bootie. Colour the scalloped edges using yellow ink.

5 Attach the booties to the card front along with two turquoise bows, then add glitter glue highlights to finish.

You will need

- white A6 card blank
- white, turquoise & yellow cardstock
- animal patterned paper
- yellow inkpad
- scallop-edged scissors
- yellow embroidery thread
- turquoise satin ribbon
- orange felt-tip pen
- die-cutting machine
- paper-piercing tool
- needle
- glitter glue
- booties template

Get Well Soon

Get Well Soon

Your step-by-step guide:

1 Follow the guide on the right to create the coloured dragon image. Apply gloss medium to his toenails and spine.

2 Cut a 10.5 cm-wide strip from the length of the A4 cardstock and score across the piece at 10.5 cm, 21 cm and 25.3 cm. Fold along the score lines to create your two-layer card blank.

3 Attach a piece of dotty paper to the front layer and pink floral paper to the second layer, leaving narrow borders.

4 Cut a tag shape from pink paper and stamp or write your greeting onto it. Layer onto a slightly larger piece of green paper, aligning the left-hand edges, then punch two small holes through both layers.

5 Tie a length of ribbon through the holes and finish with a ribbon bow, then attach the tag and the stamped image to your card front using 3D foam pads.

Colour a stamped image step-by-step

1 Swipe your cardstock with an anti-static bag then stamp your image using an embossing ink; sprinkle the embossing powder over and tip away the excess. Heat the image until the powder is melted and shiny, then cut around the image leaving a border.

2 Spritz your paint pots with water then apply a watered-down base coat to all the main areas of the image – for shading always work in one direction so that the lighter areas have the paint applied last, as it will be less intense.

3 Add fresh layers of diluted paint to any areas you want to be darker and use the paint less diluted on areas you want saturated with colour.

You will need

- selection of cardstock
- watercolour paints
- cartoon of your choice
- embossing inkpad
- black
- embossing powder
- anti-static magic bag

- patterned paper
- gloss medium
- pink organza ribbon
- heat gun
- scoreboard & bone folder
- hole punch
- 3D foam pads

Valentine's

Gorgeous

Your step-by-step guide:

1. Crease-fold a piece of white cardstock measuring 15x21 cm to create the base card.

2. Using a black inkpad, ink up the border stamp and stamp across the front of the card blank twice.

3. Stamp three love hearts using the black inkpad onto a sheet of the red paper. Cut around each heart to create a border edge of approximately 3 mm.

4. Attach the hearts onto a piece of black cardstock using double-sided tape. Cut around each heart again, this time creating a black border edge.

5. Tie a length of thread through each button. Assemble the card.

You will need

- white and black card
- heart stamps
- red patterned paper
- red buttons
- black inkpad
- wine thread

Heart to Heart

You will need

- white square card blank
- lime green cardstock
- blue organza ribbon
- green and blue eyelets
- brown inkpad
- corner rounder
- heart stamps
- heart punch

Your step-by-step guide:

1 Cut a 14 cm square of lime green cardstock. Round the corners and set an eyelet in each.

2 Stamp a heart onto the centre using brown ink. Set blue eyelets around the heart outline.

3 Stamp a border along the bottom of the panel, in brown.

4 Tie ribbon down either side of the lime green card, threading through the eyelets. Attach to your card blank to finish.

I Love You

Your step-by-step guide:

1 Create 10 pink blossoms following the instructions on the right, and leave to dry.

2 Cover the front of a white 13.5 cm-square card blank with pink cardstock and colour the edges using red ink. Cut a 12.5 cm square of patterned paper and fix to the card front.

3 Cut the image of the two birds from the patterned paper and matt onto dark brown cardstock. Attach this to the centre of the card front.

4 Stamp a sentiment onto patterned paper, trim into a rectangle and ink the edges using a red inkpad, in the same way that the blossoms were coloured. Affix in place using 3D foam pads.

5 Gently bend the petals of the blossoms to give them more dimension and secure in place around the bird image to finish.

How to colour a blossom step-by-step:

1 Die-cut small flowers from pale pink cardstock. Hold the inkpad at a 45° angle to the surface of the petals. Gently brush the inkpad from a point halfway up the petal out towards its edge. Repeat for all of the petals.

2 Hold the inkpad at a right angle to the edge of the flower's petals and press it, quite firmly, into the edge of the petal to create a darker, more solid, colouring.

3 Use the same colour of ink to stamp a small flower at the centre of the cardstock shape. Add a small dot of glitter glue to finish.

You will need

- white pink, pale pink & dark brown cardstock
- patterned paper
- floral die
- sentiments stamps
- red chalk inkpad
- dark brown inkpad
- small flower stamp
- glitter glue
- 3D foam pads

Folding Heart

Your step-by-step guide:

1. Fold a rectangle of pink cardstock to measure 30x15 cm and attach a 9 cm wide piece of patterned paper to the inside. Edge with a 1.5 cm strip of green cardstock.

2. Use the pop-up heart die to create your hearts and assemble as per the instructions.

3. Using a fineline pen, draw a broken line around the perimeter of the flat hearts.

4. Draw a heart, slightly smaller than the die-cut version, cut out and attach after folding. Attach a die-cut flower with the use of a brad.

You will need

- various cardstock
- patterned paper
- brad
- pink fineliner pen
- PVA glue
- shape cutting embossing machine
- pop-up hearts die
- flower die

Wooden Heart

Your step-by-step guide:

1   Trim a piece of kraft cardstock to measure 21x10.5 cm and creasefold to create a card blank.

2   Stamp stripes in black horizontally and vertically across the front of the card to create a chequered pattern. Ink the edges of the card using a black inkpad.

3   Trim a piece of kraft card to measure 4.5 cm square and emboss using the embossing folder.

4   Emboss a piece of green cardstock with the small square folder and ink the edges with black ink.

5   Colour the wooden heart using a red inkpad and assemble the card.

You will need

- kraft cardstock
- stripes stamp
- wooden heart
- red and black inkpads
- shape cutting embossing machine
- small square folders

With Love

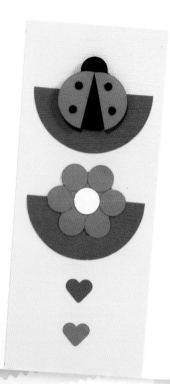

Your step-by-step guide:

1. Fix a 6 cm panel of cream cardstock to the front of the card blank. Punch out a large green cardstock circle and a green and red heart.

2. Make the ladybird's body from regular-sized punched discs of black and red card. Split the red disc in half to form the wing case.

3. Attach a mini punched disc of black card to the underside of the body for the ladybird's head. Decorate the body with tiny black punched spots.

4. Fix a mini disc of white card to the centre of a regular-sized disc of red cardstock. Attach red cardstock circles to the white disc to create a flower.

5. Cut the large green cardstock circle in half to make leaves. Assemble the card.

You will need

- white A6 card blank
- black and white cardstock
- various cardstock
- 2" circle punch
- 1/8" circle punch
- regular circle punch
- mini circle punch
- mini heart punch

Heart of Hearts

Your step-by-step guide:

1 Stamp five hearts onto white cardstock, one in red, one in pink, two in black and one in grey ink.

2 Cut out all of the stamped hearts and affix to the card front using silicone glue.

You will need

- white A6 card blank
- white cardstock
- heart stamps
- pink & red inkpad
- grey inkpad
- black inkpad
- silicone glue

General
Cards

With Love

Your step-by-step guide:

1 Fold the white card in half to form a side-fold base card.

2 Tear a rectangle of white card and pass it through the embossing folder. Matt onto torn pink and then torn purple paper. Secure together with brads in each corner, and adhere to the front of the card.

3 Tear five petal shapes and a circle for the centre of the flower in contrasting paper. Mount onto the front of the card with 3D foam pads.

4 Embellish with two torn leaf shapes and a tiny tag to write your sentiment.

You will need

- white A5 card
- variety of coloured polka dots
- 4 black brads
- pink paper string
- embossing folder
- green and white scrap card

Celebrate Flower

Your step-by-step guide:

1 Crease-fold an 8x6" piece of yellow cardstock to form the card base and draw a double black pen border. Fill the inside of the border with white paint and allow to dry.

2 Add back pen dots around the inside of the border and hand-write your greeting.

3 Stamp the arrow five times onto assorted colours of felt and cut out. Fold the stem of each over and secure using a brad layered through a paper flower.

4 Pass a length of ribbon through all the pieces and, starting at one end of the card, secure with a staple between each felt piece.

You will need

- yellow cardstock
- assorted colours of felt
- white acrylic paint
- black pen
- polka dot ribbon
- paper flowers
- pink flower brads
- black inkpad
- stapler
- arrow stamp

Sparkle Flower

Your step-by-step guide:

1 Stamp, colour and cut out the stamp of your choice. Layer a square of paper onto card. Attach to the card with foam pads.

2 Glue the circle to two daisies together, and stick to your card.

3 Dot crystals around the paper and on the stamped girl. Mount your image to your card with foam pads to finish.

You will need

- 6x6" green card blank
- stamp template of your choice
- green papers
- cardstock
- corner rounder punch
- dye inks
- large daisies
- crystals
- small circle punch

Pretty Daisy

Your step-by-step guide:

1. Trace a petal onto the chipboard and cut out. Use this as a template to cut out six more. Paint them blue and leave to dry.

2. Create a white base card and lightly brush blue paint around the edges.

3. Once the paint is dry, glue the chipboard shapes in place. Outline the petals in black pen, and use string to form the stem and flower centre.

You will need

- white textured cardstock
- string
- chipboard
- blue paint
- pencil
- black pen

Cherry Blossom Fan

Your step-by-step guide:

1   Cover the front of an A6 card blank with dark purple pearlescent cardstock. Stamp a panel of pearlescent lilac cardstock with the cherry blossom branch from the stamp set, and attach to the card.

2   Attach a 2.5 cm strip of the green side of a chosen patterned paper across the width of the card, along with a thin strip of purple striped paper.

3   Cut five pattern repeats (all slots) of the heart design onto the pink side of a different patterned paper. Cut around the edge of the cutting template to produce a shaped edge, then score and fold the cut loops, interlacing them. Cut off the loops at the righthand end of the design, at the point at which theyshould be folded.

4   Trim the bottom edges of the interlaced design to create a fan shape. Matt onto purple cardstock and add a gold handle. Lightly emboss a swirl design onto the handle using a scoring tool, then attach the fan to the card front.

5   Cut a pink flower from the first chosen patterned paper, add a pink brad to the centre, and attach to the card front to finish.

You will need

- hearts template
- 12x12" glittered patterned papers
- variety of cardstock
- oriental stamp set
- red inkpad
- pink brad

Cherry Blossom Butterflies

Your step-by-step guide:

1 From the pink patterned paper, cut the outer four slots of the entire ring of hearts. This will create just two loops to be folded for each heart. Cut around the outline of the template, then fold and interlace the loops.

2 Attach the interlaced design to pale green pearlescent cardstock, and trim. Stick to a square card blank, and trim the card to fit.

3 Cut a branch of glittered cherry blossom from a different patterned paper, and attach to the card front.

4 Cut and fold three origami butterflies (two large and one small) from the mulberry paper, and attach to the card front to finish

You will need

- hearts template
- 12x12" glittered patterned papers
- green pearlescent cardstock
- pink mulberry paper

Pretty Leaf

Your step-by-step guide:

1. Fold 15x30 cm ivory cardstock in half to form a mountain-fold base card.

2. Paint a 13 cm square onto purple paper using a wet paintbrush, and tease out. Adhere to the card front.

3. Paint a 9 cm square onto pink paper and tease out.

4. Prick stitch holes onto the pink paper square and draw in faux stitches.

5. Paint a leaf shape onto lime green paper and tease out, fold and pass through a corrugator. Open, and adhere to your card.

6. Cut a long strip of the yellow paper and tie into a bow. Adhere to the front of the card.

You will need

- ivory cardstock
- variety of coloured paper
- dry stick glue
- paper-piercing tool
- silver pen
- paper corrugator
- pink inkpad

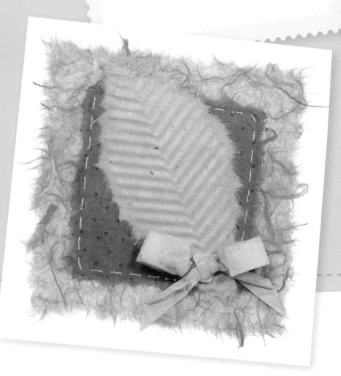

A Quaint Note

Your step-by-step guide:

1   Cover the card front with patterned paper, distressing the edges with chosen ink.

2   Cut a greeting panel from the patterned paper and attach to the centre of the card.

3   Position the paper flowers down the left-hand side of the panel, making sure the large brown flower is centered over the brown flourish.

4   Add the remaining paper flowers to the bottom righthand corner of the panel, before embellishing each with an adhesive pearl and brown square buttons.

You will need

- cream 115 mm-squarecard blank
- brown square buttons
- patterned papers
- coloured paper flowers
- blue and brown adhesive pearls
- inkpad

Oriental Lantern

Your step-by-step guide:

1 Create a 23⁄4 x 7 1⁄4" card blank from red cardstock. Using the oriental templates, cut out a row of three tea bagfolding papers, leaving narrow borders around them. Fix to the centre of the card blank.

2 Place a lantern image and two of the symbols from the template sheet onto pearlescent cardstock. Colour in the lantern and the borders with a black gel pen.

3 Trim around each image, leaving a narrow border around the lantern image, and fix to each square on the card. The characters should be fixed flat with double-sided tape and the lantern should be raised with 3D foam pads.

You will need

- oriental templates
- red cardstock
- pale yellow pearlescent cardstock
- 3D foam pads

Cherry on Top

Your step-by-step guide:

1 Print off a cupcake template and cut out the large cupcake topper. Matt with silver mirri card and green cardstock.

2 Line the inside of an aperture card blank with cupcake backing paper so that it is visible through the aperture. Create a dashed line around the outside of the aperture with a glitter pen.

3 Mount the matted cupcake image over the aperture. Create a slit towards the bottom of the card spine and wrap with a length of red ribbon, tying in a knot at the front.

4 Add gloss medium to the cherry on the cupcake and set aside to dry properly to finish.

You will need

- cupcake template
- silver mirri card
- green cardstock
- white aperture card
- red ribbon
- gloss medium
- green glitter pen
- 3D foam pads

White Dragonflies

Your step-by-step guide:

1 Trim two co-ordinating patterned papers to 11 cm and 9 cm square, layer together and matt with maroon cardstock, leaving a wide border around the edges.

2 Wrap green ribbon around the bottom of the panel and tie into a knot. Attach to the front of a white 13 cm-square card blank.

3 Punch three dragonflies from dotty paper, and attach to the centre of the card using 3D foam pads. Highlight the dragonfly bodies with gems to finish.

You will need

- white card blank
- maroon cardstock
- patterned papers
- green ribbon
- adhesive gems
- dragonfly punch

Bouquet

Your step-by-step guide:

1   Cover a square card blank with
    gold paper. Tear a square of orange
    handmade paper, ink the edges brown
    and adhere to the centre of the card.

2   Adhere a light orange skeleton leaf
    to the centre of the orange
    handmade square.

3   Create a mini bouquet of flowers by
    cutting three lengths of craft wire,
    bending into shape and gluing pearl
    flower heads to the top of the length.
    Tie a brown ribbon bow at the
    bottom and attach to the leaf.

You will need

- gold paper
- craft pack
- brown inkpad
- orange pearly flowers
- craft wire
- brown ribbon

Fields of Flowers

Your step-by-step guide:

1 Stamp the flower swirl in the centre of a cream card blank, heat-embossing for definition if you prefer.

2 Cover the front of the card with a 135 mm square of blue cardstock, removing a 50 mm square from its centre to create a frame.

3 Cut a 125 mm square from the reverse of patterned paper, and trim diagonally to make four triangles.

4 Lay each triangle onto the card front and fold the centre point of each triangle out to the edge, revealing the blue cardstock and the stamped flower swirl.

5 Decorate the frame with paper flowers, and embellish with adhesive pearls to finish.

You will need

- cream 145 mm-square card blank
- patterned paper
- blue cardstock
- clear stamps
- brown and blue adhesive pearls
- brown, blue and latte paper flowers
- chalk inkpad

Shake a Tail Feather

Your step-by-step guide:

1. Trim orange paper to fit the front of a white card blank, edge with distress ink and attach.

2. Stamp your image onto white cardstock using a brown inkpad and colour using marker pens. Add gloss medium and die-cut into a scalloped circle. Matt with a slightly larger scalloped circle die-cut from blue paper and attach to the right-hand side of the card blank.

3. Tie a ribbon bow and attach to the card, along with paper flowers. Using the jewel template, make a flourish on the left-hand side of the card using pearls and gems.

4. Cut a wavy rectangle from orange spotty paper and a sentiment strip from white and blue pearlised cardstock. Edge with your choice of ink, assemble then stamp with your sentiment using another choice of ink to create your insert.

You will need

- white A6 pearlised card blank
- white cardstock
- marker pens
- brown inkpad
- jewel template
- gloss medium
- brown gingham ribbon

- patterned paper and co-ordinating cardstock
- variety of inkpads
- circle and rectangle dies
- white self-adhesive pearls and blue tear gems
- duck stamp
- cherry paper flowers

Purple Flowers

Your step-by-step guide:

1. Cut purple cardstock to fit the front of a 15 cm square white card blank, leaving a narrow border around the edges.

2. Stamp the larger corner violet image onto pale lilac cardstock using distress ink and spray with water. Once dry, trim to measure 13.5 x 7.5 cm and adhere across the bottom of the card.

3. Trim a piece of white embossed cardstock to fit the top half of the card, attach and use a die-cut purple border to cover the join.

4. Stamp your image onto white cardstock using black ink, colour using marker pens and heat-emboss with embossing powder.

5. Die-cut your image into a circle and mount onto a scalloped circle die-cut from purple cardstock. Mount in the centre of the card to finish.

You will need

- flower stamp set
- white embossed cardstock
- crest cardstock
- circle and scalloped circle dies
- set of marker pens

- foamboard
- black inkpad
- distress ink
- purple and light purple cardstock
- embossing powders

Cutie Pie

You will need

- white and pink cardstock
- white cotton fabric
- patterned paper
- cage stamp
- pink ribbon
- black inkpad

- distress ink
- marker pens
- pinking shears
- brayer
- scalloped edge punch
- glue gel

Your step-by-step guide:

1   Create a white 12.5 cm-square base card. Cut a piece of pink cardstock to 12x13 cm, punch a border down the right and affix.

2   Cut a piece of patterned paper to 10x11.5 cm, tie a piece of ribbon around it, tie in a knot then secure to the card front.

3   Stamp the cage image onto white cotton fabric.

4   Using a brayer, colour the fabric with distress inks.

5   Add detail to the image using marker pens and trim using pinking shears. Matt onto fabric and trim using pinking shears. Add a piece of cardstock to the back of the image panel, then attach it to the card front at an angle using glue gel.

Zigzag Patches

Your step-by-step guide:

1. Matt a 14 cm-square piece of white cardstock onto patterned paper leaving a narrow border.

2. Using zigzag scissors, cut three 2.5 cm-wide strips of patterned paper, one 6.5 cm long, one 9 cm long and one 11.5 cm long. Attach to the cardstock panel.

3. Add a zigzag stitch across the three patterned paper strips.

4. Zigzag-stitch around the edges of the white cardstock panel then secure to the card front to finish.

You will need

- white 15.5 cm-squarecard blank
- white cardstock
- patterned paper
- zigzag scissors
- sewing machine
- sewing thread
- silicone glue

Pink Zinnia

Your step-by-step guide:

1 Stamp a border using embossing enamel onto a pink 15.2 cm-square card blank. Smudge with brown chalk. Apply vivid chalk colours to pink cardstock large enough for two flowers.

2 Stamp two flowers onto pink cardstock using watermark ink. Dust with embossing enamel and heat. Cut out one full flower and trim away the outer petals of the second. Stamp and emboss a flower centre using embossing enamel and trim.

3 Curl the petals of the smaller flower around a pencil.

4 Wrap a piece of ribbon around the card front, above the stamped border, and tie in a knot.

5 Assemble the two flowers and affix to the card front. Add glue to the flower centre and dust with mica fragments. Allow to dry, then attach using 3D foam pads.

You will need

- pink and brown cardstock
- flower stamp
- embossing enamels
- mica fragments
- watermark inkpad
- brown ribbon
- brown, red, orange and purple chalk
- 3D foam pads

House

Your step-by-step guide:

1. Using the window pane shape die with the magnetic window positioned in the top corner, cut your card blank from yellow colour core cardstock.

2. Use the same die to cut a white piece of card, trim around the window shape to create a frame and glue into position.

3. Take a piece of orange card and use a ruler and pencil to draw a roof shape, using the partly made card as your size guide. Cut out the roof and secure into position with double-sided tape.

4. Matt a purple cardstock rectangle onto white card and add a large brad to resemble a door knob. Fix your door onto the front of the card using foam pads for added dimension.

5. Finish by attaching concertinafolded patterned paper to the inside of the card to resemble curtains, and adding a thin rectangle of card to the roof section to make a chimney.

You will need

- colour core cardstock
- shape cutting machine
- window pane shaper
- brad
- foam pads

Double Hanging Flower

Your step-by-step guide:

1 Fold a 10x20 cm rectangle of purple cardstock and matt the inside with white paper to create your card blank.

2 Attach a 5 cm band of patterned paper to the bottom of your card, then add a 1 cm wide strip of yellow card.

3 Open the card flat and turn it over. With a ruler and pencil draw a line 3 cm from each edge, a line 4 cm from the top edge and another line 5 cm from the bottom edge.

4 Use a sharp craft knife and ruler to cut out the rectangle that you have created.

5 Take a 13 cm length of nylon thread and attach to the inside of your card with tape.

6 Die-cut four flower shapes and stick them back-to-back using PVA glue, sandwiching the thread between the layers.

7 Using the scallop square die and green cardstock, create a scalloped shape and trim before attaching to the right-hand side of the card.

You will need

- colour cardstock
- patterned paper
- embossing machine
- flowers die
- scallop square die
- nylon thread
- ribbon

Stroke of Midnight

Your step-by-step guide:

1 Score and fold lilac cardstock in half widthways to make an A5 card blank. Cut choice of decorative paper to fit the card front, matt with silver mirror card and attach.

2 Cut a strip of silver mirror card and die-cut a swirly pattern in the centre. Attach the negative to the left-hand side of the card.

3 Make a clock face using the template, clock hands dies and peel-off numbers, and attach to the left-hand side of the card front with 3D foam. Decorate the inside of the card with decorative paper.

4 Score and fold a 29x21 cm piece of purple cardstock widthways into four equal panels. Cut a circle in the middle of the central panels, and decorate the outer two panels with silver mirror card, decorative paper and silver die-cut swirls.

5 Use frosted acetate to make another clock face and attach to the central panels with chain links, to dangle in the aperture.

6 Attach the inner card to the outer A5 card by the two outer panels only. Finish with flatbacked pearls.

You will need

- purple and lilac cardstock
- silver mirror card
- die cut swirls
- clock hands template
- decorative paper
- flat-backed gems
- silver brads
- silver chain links

Pink Rose

Your step-by-step guide:

1 Crease-fold a 13.5 cm square piece of white cardstock to create your card base.

2 Cut a piece of lavender cardstock to fit the card front, leaving a narrow border around the edges.

3 Use a scoring tool to score horizontal and vertical lines onto the lavender panel and add small drops lavender pearls at each intersection as shown. Wrap ribbon around the bottom of the panel and fix to the card.

4 Cut small squares of green and white card and layer together.

5 Punch several heart shapes from pink cardstock and paint with pink pearls. Once dry, layer up the heart shapes and push a brad through all the layers, shaping the petals in your hand to form a rose shape.

6 Cut leaves from green cardstock, trim fringing around the edges and stick behind the rose. Mount the finished flower onto the layered squares, then secure to the centre of the card.

Strips of Scraps

Your step-by-step guide:

1 Crease-fold a 8 1/2x5 1/2" piece of cream cardstock to create a side-fold card blank.

2 Cut a 4x5 1/4" panel from scrap paper and cover with 4" strips of leftover patterned papers. Use strips of varying width and try to keep the colours balanced.

3 Using a sewing machine, stitch across the panel, using a combination of straight and zigzag stitches of different widths.

4 Round the corners and adhere to the card front using double-sided tape.

You will need

- cream cardstock
- patterned paper strips
- pink thread
- sewing machine
- corner-rounder punch